THE

MISSING

LINK

- IN THEOLOGY -

Second Edition

Julio A. Rodriguez

THE MISSING LINK

- In Theology -

ISBN: 978-0-9779349-7-3

Original Spanish Title:

"El Eslabón Perdido – en la Teología"

Translated by: Frank Mercado

All Scripture quotations, unless otherwise indicated, are taken from the King James Version of the Holy Bible, 1850

Cover designed by: Luz Angela Gonzalez
Printed in United States of America

Published by:
Editorial Nueva Vida, Inc.
53-21 37 Ave., Woodside, NY, 11377
Ph: 718-205-5111   www.editorialnuevavida.net

- First Edition Published in September 2007
- Second Edition Published in July 2009

"Where sin abounded,

Grace

Did much more abound"

(Roman 5:20)

"...And when he had opened the book, he found the place where it was written,

The Spirit of the Lord is upon me, because he hath anointed me to preach the gospel to the poor; he hath sent me to heal the brokenhearted, to preach deliverance to the captives, and recovering of sight to the blind, to set at liberty them that are bruised,

To preach the acceptable year of the Lord."

Luke 4:17b-19

DEDICATION:

To the blessed Holy Spirit, as He has honored me with the precious task of communicating these truths; and He has taken me from nothing and placed me in His service, for the glory of the Lord Jesus and our heavenly Father.

To every human being from every country, tribe, tongue, or nation, wherever they may be found, so that, through the goodness of God, they may understand the true significance of His grace offered freely because of the price paid by the Lord Jesus Christ through His sacrifice of atonement that He alone, in love, in His own body on the cross of Calvary finished, and the Father accepted and was able to make peace with all humanity and justify all before Him, according to His perfect will and holiness.

With love and by His mercy,

Julio Rodriguez

Pastor Julio Rodriguez

The Missing Link in Theology

The Missing Link in Theology

My prayer to the Lord is
That all who read this book
Have an open mind
And analyze all the points made
With their Bible, as they are presented,
And may the Spirit of Truth,
The Holy Spirit,
Be their guide in all truth.
(J.R.)

PREFACE

The time is 11:15 in the morning this last Sunday of June, 2005. We are experiencing the glorious presence of the Lord. The Lord encourages us with a Word from Isaiah 60.

It reads:

> "Arise, shine: for thy light is come, and the glory of the Lord is risen upon thee. For, behold, the darkness shall cover the earth, and gross darkness the people: but the Lord shall arise upon thee, and his glory shall be seen upon thee. And the Gentiles shall come to thy light, and kings to the brightness of thy rising" (Isaiah 60: 1-3)[1]

As the service continues, our assistant pastor for youth is scheduled to preach. The people are enjoying the move of the Holy Spirit in a special manner.

Our inner ear is attentive and we sense a receptive attitude. Suddenly our speaker cites a biblical passage found in the book of Esther:

> "For if thou altogether holdest thy peace at this time, then shall there enlargement and deliverance

---

[1] All Scripture quotations, unless otherwise indicated, are taken from the King James Version of the Holy Bible, 1850

arise to the Jews from another place: but thou and thy father's house shall be destroyed: and who knoweth whether thou art come to the kingdom for such a time as this? (Esther 4:14)

At this time the message becomes a personal conversation with the Holy Spirit that brings to remembrance the many ways that He had been speaking to me.

I feel compelled to write on this theme, though truthfully, I'd rather not. It's very conflictive. I identify with Moses when God instructed him to return to Egypt and present himself before Pharaoh.

I asked, **Why me Lord?** You have great and influential preachers and servants; world renowned. Why can't you send one of them to at least begin this message, and then I can join them?

The Lord is patient and merciful and doesn't become angry with me; but instead gives me some reasons in answer to the question I had for Him.

To begin with, I'm reminded that "If a grain of wheat goes not into the ground and dies, it remains alone, but if it dies, it then bears much fruit." The word "dies" is what causes my anguish.

I've believed that I left all to serve Him; and in a manner of speaking, died to my ego and personal desires, but the Lord indicates there is still an area He expects me to die in: To feel accepted, loved, and received; in other words, being secure in the ministry.

He expects me to surrender my expectations and only wait on Him as His plan for these crucial times unfolds.

A part of Queen Esther's response was

> "And so will I go in unto the king, which is not according to the law; and if I perish, I perish." (Esther 4:16)

I still hear the preacher's voice, "This is the time, the *"Kairos"* of God". **This is the time!**

The situation is this: It has been several years since the Holy Spirit stirs within me an analysis of Scripture that is unconventional; that does not coincide with what I usually hear and examine from anointed people used by God with signs and wonders around the world.

It would seem obvious to state: This is a thorny and controversial subject

The Lord has spoken to me of a new form of "Tradition" that has supplanted the truth. It is a tradition so deeply rooted that is it difficult to speak or think on it without associating this as established truth.

It's a tradition that is surely the result of a powerful, deceptive satanic strategy that has affected and discredited Christianity to the degree that today we have very little credibility in a lost and needy world. This tradition has such a radical perspective on human salvation that we lose everything concerning the fear of God, and His dealings with mankind.

Some questions need an answer. Among them are:

1. What happens to a person that dies without receiving the Lord Jesus Christ as his personal Saviour if the message of salvation has not been heard by him? Will there be a remote possibility that God allows him to enter heaven?

2. What happens to people that although they believe in Jesus, still continue religious practices that are an abomination to God, but nevertheless live in sincere faith with Christian love and generosity in the hope the Lord will receive them in heaven on that day?

3. What shall happen to those who claim to be Christians, but their testimonies demonstrate otherwise? Will they enter heaven in spite of this?

It would seem obvious to state: This is a thorny and controversial subject. The easy path would be to accept what we have heard and possibly learned traditionally, not withstanding, the Lord continues speaking to me: It's time for **ALL** the truth. Now is the time!

Two weeks ago, the Lord challenged me. He asked me: are you willing to risk your reputation in proclamation of the truth?

He reminded me that the Lord Jesus, during the times of ministry that He was "popular", always told the truth (though it may have been unpopular). Consequentially, on many occasions He was threatened with violence.

My answer, after a momentary reflection, was an unconditional yes; though I could imagine the attitude and severe criticism of some who would not comprehend.

For a long time I've waited for others to enter a discourse on this theme, be it a local, national, or international figure.
I diligently searched the internet to see if someone had taken the initiative to discuss this theme, but as of today there has been no answer. I've consulted and researched many books and seen that this theme is ignored.

The many Bible commentaries have excluded this and no one has dared to confront this Christian tradition.

The Lord would repeat today:

> "If a grain of wheat falls not into the ground and dies it remains alone, but if it dies it shall bring forth much fruit."

The Holy Spirit would reveal to me that, although in my ministry I've always attempted to work with a team and seek advice in all I felt necessary; in what He was now asking me, I had to go alone. To recall our Lord Jesus Christ, He was alone as He obeyed and went to the cross. No one was able to share this with Him; Apostles nor followers, not even his own mother was able.

The Lord has asked me to sacrifice my "Isaac" and expects my obedience, as did Abraham obey, though I do not understand God's motive for this request.

In my indecision, the Lord reminds me that He will always be with me, and that He will never abandon me in any time of persecution. Though I walk through the fire, He will provide all the protection I need to keep me whole. I should confide in Him in all the times of trial, and not fear anything or anyone, as He is my Savior.

For a long time I've waited for others to enter a discourse on this theme, be it a local, national, or international figure

The Lord inquires to everyone:

Who else is there that is willing to give up great popularity in their sphere of influence in Christianity to suffer persecution, for the cause of truth?

ACCOMODATING THE TRUTH: A FORM OF NEW TRADITION.

"A son honoreth his father and
a servant his
master: if then I
be a father, where
is mine honor?
And if I be a
master, **where is
my
fear**? Saith
the Lord of
hosts unto
you," (Malachi 1:6)

"He that walketh in his uprightness **feareth the Lord:** but he that is perverse in his ways despiseth him" (Proverbs 14:2)

"**The fear of the Lord** is the beginning of wisdom" (Proverbs 9:10)

"By humility and **fear of the Lord** are riches, and honor, and life" (Proverbs 22:4)

The Gospel of Mark relates how Jesus confronted the Jews and the religious people of his time, condemning the rituals they had established as valid before God's eyes.

He said:

> "Well hath Isaiah prophesied of you hypocrites, as it is written, this people honoreth me with their lips, but their heart is far from me."

> **"Howbeit in vain do they worship me**, teaching for doctrines the commandments of men. For laying aside the commandment of God, ye hold the tradition of men…"

> "…Making the word of God of none effect through your tradition, which you have delivered…" (Mark 7:6-8a, 13a)

The Lord has revealed to me that this new **"tradition"** that has been accepted in these last generations are **thoughts and doctrinal ideas** that substituted the veracity of the message of God given in His Word.

We should not be surprised that Christianity has greatly lost its powerful influence in the world to the degree it is considered that we now live in the "post- Christian Era".

Much thought that is accepted in the Christian world has been permitted to take shape and provoked a falling away of faith in the majority, and a sense of frustration in many others.

> We should not be surprised that Christianity has greatly lost its powerful influence in the world

One train of thought is the following:

"There are two forms of interpreting the Bible and both, though they are contradictory, will agree as to what each has to say." (This is similar to humanistic relativism: "The truth is relative and depends on the interpretation you attribute to it).

This expression is usually used by those attempting to understand either the **Calvinist** or the **Arminian** viewpoints, which we shall further elaborate on:

A brief description of the 5 premises of Calvinism and the 5 of Arminianism

 **FIRST POINT**

CALVINIST: Total Depravation or Total Inability

Due to the fall, man is incapable of believing in the gospel of salvation on his own. A sinner is deaf, blind, and dead to the things of God. His heart is deceitful and desperately wicked.

He hasn't a free will and is enslaved by his evil nature; subsequently, he is not able to choose for good over evil in a spiritual sense. It then follows that it requires more than the insistence of the Holy Spirit for a sinner to come to Christ.

Regeneration is necessary, by which the Holy Spirit gives new life and a new nature. Faith is not man's contribution to his salvation; but is rather part of this same gift of salvation.

ARMINIAN: Human Capacity, Self will or Free will

Although man's will was seriously compromised by the fall, his natural state has not been left in total spiritual abandonment. Every sinner is graciously afforded the opportunity to repent and believe, by God, without any interference in each individual decision by Him.

Every sinner possesses free will and their eternal destiny is determined by this use of choice. The freedom mankind enjoys consists in our ability to choose for good over bad, in spiritual matters.

Our will is not enslaved by our sinful nature. Every sinner has the power to cooperate with the Holy Spirit and be regenerated, or resist the grace of God and perish.

The lost person needs the assistance of the Holy Spirit, but does not have to be regenerated before he is able to believe; leaving the Holy Spirit to begin His work of regeneration, progressing and perfecting by sanctification after a sinner surrenders his life to God. A person contributes faith to his salvation.

SECOND POINT.

CALVINIST: Unconditional Election

The selection by God of certain individuals for salvation, before the foundation of the world, rested only on His own sovereign will.

This selection of any particular sinners was not based on the foreknowledge of the response or obedience of an individual, but on the contrary, God gives the faith and repentance each person he has elected needs. Their responses are the result, not the reason, of God's election.

Therefore the election was not determined nor had a condition of any virtuous quality or action foresaw by God in any man. God enables all those chosen by his sovereign will, to accept Christ by the power of the Holy Spirit.

ARMINIAN: Conditional Election

The election that God has made of certain individuals for salvation, before the foundation of the world, has been based on the foreknowledge of God, in that He knows what their response to the call of salvation will be.
God has chosen only those whom He knew would freely choose to believe the gospel and receive Christ.

This election is determined and conditional on an action.

Therefore the act of deciding to believe in Christ, rather than God's selection of a particular sinner, is the cause for salvation ultimately.

THIRD POINT

CALVINIST: Limited Atonement or Partial Redemption

The work of redemption completed by Christ had the intention of saving only those persons God has elected to save, and also assure the salvation of these elected ones. The atoning death of Christ then only pays the price for the sin of those elected.

In addition to forgetting their sins, Christ's redemption provided everything for their salvation, including the faith that would unite them. The gift of faith is perfectly applied by the Holy Spirit to all the elect Christ died for, and the finished work guarantees their salvation.

ARMINIAN: General Atonement or Universal Redemption

The work of redemption by Christ has made it possible for all mankind to be saved, but has no guarantee for any one particular person. Although Christ died for all and everyone can be saved, only those who believe in Him are saved.

His death has allowed God to forgive the sins of anyone, with the condition of faith in Christ. Redemption through Christ is applied only when a person accepts this salvation.

FOURTH POINT

Calvinist: Irresistible Grace or The Call of the Holy Spirit

In addition to the general call to salvation made to all those who hear the gospel, the Holy Spirit extends an inner special call to the elect, and inevitably saves them.

The general call (which is made to call men without preference) can be rejected, but the particular call (which is only for the elect) cannot be rejected and always leads to conversion. In this particular call the Holy Spirit brings sinners to Christ in an irresistible manner.

The Holy Spirit is not limited by human volition neither depends on any cooperation by man., to accomplish the work of salvation in mankind.

The Holy Spirit graciously obliges those elect sinners to cooperate, believe, and repent, in liberty and willingly to Christ. The grace of God is invincible. It never fails to save to those whom it has been offered by God.

ARMINIAN: The Holy Spirit can be resisted.

The Holy Spirit makes an inner call, to all those who hear the invitation of the gospel; but since each person has free will; it is possible to reject the Holy Spirit and this call. Regeneration cannot occur by the Holy Spirit until there is faith.

Faith (which is man's contribution) precedes and makes possible the new birth. Therefore, the free will of man can limit the ability of the Holy Spirit to apply the finished work of Christ.

He can only rescue those who allow him. When a response is not adequate, the Holy Spirit can give no life to a sinner. In conclusion, God's grace is not invincible. It can be, and frequently is, resisted and frustrated by man.

FIFTH POINT:

CALVINIST: The saints will persevere
All those elected by God, redeemed by Christ and that have accepted the faith given them by the Holy Spirit, are eternally secure in their salvation. The power of God sustains their faith and they all persevere until the end.

ARMINIAN: One can fall from grace.

All those who have believed and been saved, can lose their salvation if they do not retain their faith in Christ and persevere until the end.

>>> **As we can appreciate**, the discussion of the offer of salvation in Christ, unfortunately, has been framed within the context of two polarizing positions: **Limited atonement versus unlimited atonement.**

Typically, those in favor of one or the other theological current focus on the portions of scripture they deem favorable to their position.

We are surprised as we see how secular relativism has infiltrated Christianity, in considering morality does not exist, it states nothing is correct or incorrect but all depends on the angle in which it is seen.

This form of thinking is not right; as it is clear there is ONE truth, impregnable and indestructible

It's as if we say that if you believe in something and your conscience does not offend you, that is correct for you, though it may be another person has a diametrically opposed opinion as yours, if they believe and their conscience accuses them not, they're also correct.

This form of thinking is not right; as it is clear there is ONE truth, impregnable and indestructible; and there should be no confusion as to it. Jesus Christ is the truth and He alone can reveal the mysteries of this life. We are 100% sure that God has revealed this to all humanity.

The Bible declares:

> "The secret things belong unto the Lord our God: but those things which are revealed belong unto us and to our children forever, that we may do all the words of this law." (Deuteronomy 29:29)

And also:

> "My people are destroyed for lack of
> knowledge"   (Hosea 4:6)

In a manner of speaking, those whose background has been grounded in Calvinist thought believe they form part of an elect group chosen by God and it matters not what they do or don't do, heaven is certain for them;

In contrast, those taught the Arminian current believe heaven is not assured to anyone as it depends on one maintaining himself in holiness and not fall (habitual sin).

When someone comes to the foot of the cross and receives salvation through grace, that person is normally instructed in a church and in a short time begins to reflect on their actions, manner of speech, etc., and the stream of thought in the "indoctrination" to Christianity.

When our **everyday citizen** analyzes his existence and begins to question what his destiny will be after he leaves this world, they normally seek answers in religion and eventually are submerged in the sea of contradictory opinions and beliefs.

We are 100% sure that God has revealed this to all humanity.

The discovery of the multitude of religions and sects will leave them uncertain as to who actually knows and practices the truth (and sometimes will question if absolute truth really exists).

Normally, in the Christian world we speak of Christ and his work of redemption; but we are constantly accusing each other (as it depends in the manner we comprehend or have been taught the Scriptures); and instead of an example of love to this world, unity and peace, we confuse those coming to our churches for answers.

Although we preach Jesus, we do not live by the words of Jesus.

We can recall the question of the Lord on one occasion:

> And why call ye me, Lord, Lord **and do not** the things which I say? (Luke 6: 46)

What shall we do?

First and fundamentally, let us return to the Word. We should recognize we are not walking as God would have us and make the necessary adjustments.

What were we told and believed that the Word of God does not prove? Was our belief based on the influence of someone important, or learned?

Are we faithful or not, to the integrity of the Word of God?

Let us recall the words of the Apostle Paul

> "But the natural man receiveth not the things of the Spirit of God: for they are foolishness unto him: neither can he know them, because they are spiritually discerned. But he that is spiritual judges all things, yet he himself is judged of no man." (1 Cor. 2 14-15)

We should be **very cautious** in our Bible study and note the importance of seeking **scriptural equilibrium of God** in any doctrine. This will help us avoid all extremes that inadvertently frustrate believers instead of edifying, as we walk with the Lord.

Let us learn to see the Bible as a whole and not dwell solely on a small portion (especially when a truth is not that crystal clear or is ambiguous). God desires that we come to the knowledge of all the truth.

King David said:

> "Come, ye children, hearken unto me: I will teach you **the fear of the Lord**. What man is he that desireth life? And loveth many days that he may see good? Keep thy tongue from evil, and thy lips from speaking guile. Depart from evil, and do good; seek peace and pursue it."
> (Psalm 34: 11-14)

The Lord has made known to me that in what the world labels "post-Christian era", He calls this the

"ERA OF CHRISTIAN RENOVATION"

Allowing us to understand there are glorious times ahead for the church of God on this earth.

I Pray to our Lord that we all may participate in this move of God over all the face of the earth

A "Key" Word

In the gospel of John, we find a word that may greatly illuminate our understanding, Jesus said:

> "I am the way, the truth, and the life: no man cometh unto the Father, but **by** me." (John 14:6)

The key word we wish to analyze is
"BY" (Gr. *"dia"*)

This word has <u>two meanings</u>. On the one hand, it means **"across"** or **"through"**, and another meaning is **"because of"** or "as a result of what has been done."

We will verify that **both meanings** are valid in the redemptory work of Jesus

Normally we accept only the **first meaning** as correct. Traditionally we understand that Jesus said "no one comes to the Father but **through** me".

- With this interpretation starts our inquiry regarding the provision made by God for those who reside in a remote corner of our planet, and have not heard of Christ.

- They live a "normal" life depending on the mores of the culture in their native land; however, **how can they go to heaven if they die without anyone speaking to them of Christ?**

Let us take notice that if we analyze the verse with the **second meaning** of the word "by", we may give it the significance: **"no one can come to the Father if not "because" of me".**

In other words, Jesus tells us that had He not completed the work of redemption successfully, humanity would never have been able to enter heaven.
Not even King David or Abraham would enter.

Jesus stated at that time that the just souls waited in **"Abraham's Bosom"** (Luke 16:22) and were not risen to heaven unless Jesus conquered Satan and restored all things.

Let us analyze what happened:

The Word also tells us that during the time the body of

ADAM	CHRIST
He did not exist (Genesis2:5);	Eternally existed (John1:1)
Was made from dust (Gen. 2:7) and was given dominion (Gen. 1:28; 2:19)	Who, existing in the nature of God, ... He emptied Himself, having taken the nature of a slave ... (Philipp 2: 6-8) *(ALT -Analitical Literal Translation)*
Lived in paradise, without strife, without pressure, without attacks (Gen.2:15-16);	Lived in dangerous times; suffered persecution and violence (from the time he entered his mother's womb there were threats of death). In all, He was obedient unto the hour of death, death on a cross.
Moreover, with all this allowed himself to be overcome by the evil one and disobeyed	
In the midst of the abundance, he lost everything (Gen. 3: 23-24)	In the scornful death of the cross He gained redemption of all Adam had lost; defeating Satan and all evil forces (Colossians. 2:15)

Jesus lay in the tomb, the Lord **"went and preached to all those souls in chains"** (1 Peter 3:19);

Ephesians 4 declares:

> "Wherefore he saith, when he ascended up on high, he led captivity captive, and gave gifts unto men..." (Ephesians 4:8-10)

Those who died with the hope that God is faithful to His promise are no longer in Abraham's Bosom; **Jesus brought them to heaven!**

We are also told that Jesus, **in his overcoming and completed work:**

> "God also hath highly exalted him, and gives him a name which is above every name: That at the name of Jesus every knee should bow, of things in heaven, and things in earth, and things

under the earth; And that every tongue should confess that Jesus Christ is Lord, to the glory of God the Father. (Phil 2: 9-11)

"Who is gone into heaven, and is on the right hand of God; **angels and authorities and powers being made subject unto him.**
   (1Peter 3:22)

"And one of the elders saith unto me, Weep not: behold, the lion of the tribe of Judah, the root of David, **hath prevailed** to open the book, and to loose the seven seals thereof ..."

"...And every creature which is in heaven, and on the earth, and under the earth, and such as are in the sea, and all that are in them, heard I saying, Blessing, and honor, and glory, and power, **be unto him that sitteth upon the throne, and unto the Lamb** forever and ever. And the four beasts said, Amen. And the four and twenty elders fell down and worshipped him that liveth forever and ever."
   (Revelation 5:5-14)

We read a verse in the Bible that reveals a great truth and allow us understand there was also **something that would occur in heaven** that would have to reconciled, and was fulfilled with the death of Jesus on the cross.

It states:

"And, having made peace through the blood of his cross, by him **to reconcile** all things unto himself; by him, I say, whether they be **things in earth**, or **things in heaven**." (Colossians 1:20)

WHAT WAS THIS?

The Bible declares there was once a rebellion in heaven and the protagonist was none other than Satan, who was a cherub, **"perfect in all his ways from the day he was created, until sin was found in him."** (Ezekiel 28:15); And that he was cast out of heaven.

ISAIAH SAYS:

"Yet thou shalt be brought down to hell, to the sides of the pit."(Isaiah14:15)

[For the benefit of the reader, we include these passages that narrate what transpired, in Ezekiel 28 and Isaiah 14]

EZEKIEL 28: 12b -19

"Thus sayeth the Lord God; Thou sealest up the sum, full of wisdom, and perfect in beauty. Thou hast been in Eden the garden of God; every precious stone was thy covering, the sardius, topaz, and the diamond, the beryl, the onyx, and the jasper, the sapphire, the emerald, and the carbuncle, and gold: the workmanship of thy tabrets and thy pipes was prepared in thee in the day that thou wast created:"

"Thou art the anointed cherub that covereth; and I have set thee so: thou wast upon the holy mountain of God; thou hast walked up and down in the midst of the stones of fire. Thou wast perfect in thy ways from the day that thou wast created, till iniquity was found thee."

"By the multitude of thy merchandise they have filled the midst of thee with violence, and thou hast sinned: therefore I will cast thee as profane out of the mountain of God: and I will destroy thee, O covering cherub, from the midst of the stones of fire. Thine heart was lifted up because of thy beauty, thou hast corrupted thy wisdom by reason of thy brightness: I will cast thee to the ground, I will lay thee before kings, that they may behold thee."

"Thou hast defiled thy sanctuaries by the multitude of thy iniquities, by the iniquity of thy traffic; therefore will I bring forth a fire from the midst of thee, it shall devour thee, and I will bring thee to ashes upon the earth in the sight of all them that behold thee. All they that know thee among the people shall be astonished at thee: thou shalt be a terror, and never shalt thou be anymore."

ISAIAH 14: 12-15

> "How art thou fallen from heaven, O Lucifer, son of the morning! How art thou cut to the ground, which didst weaken the nations! For thou hast said in thine heart, I will ascend into heaven, I will exalt my throne above the stars of God: I will sit also upon the mount of the congregation, in the sides of the north: I will ascend above the heights of the clouds; I will be like the most High. Yet thou shalt be brought down to hell, to the sides of the pit."

When Jesus died on the cross, there was great peace in heaven. The consequence of God's judgment against Lucifer may have appeared unjust or too severe. **We now know that God is perfect in His judgments**.

Jesus demonstrates it was possible to obey God always, even in our most terrible moments.

Jesus, with perfect obedience, restored the true significance of God's justice.

Lucifer rebelled and disobeyed.

Adam disobeyed and sinned;

Jesus always obeyed and conquered.

OBEDIENCE BRINGS
VICTORY AND PEACE!

BELIEVE, CONFIDE and **OBEY** should be impressionable words in our life.

In the following chapter, we will analyze a central doctrine that attempts to explain why human beings disobey and commit sin.

A Doctrine that has influenced history: "THE ORIGINAL SIN"

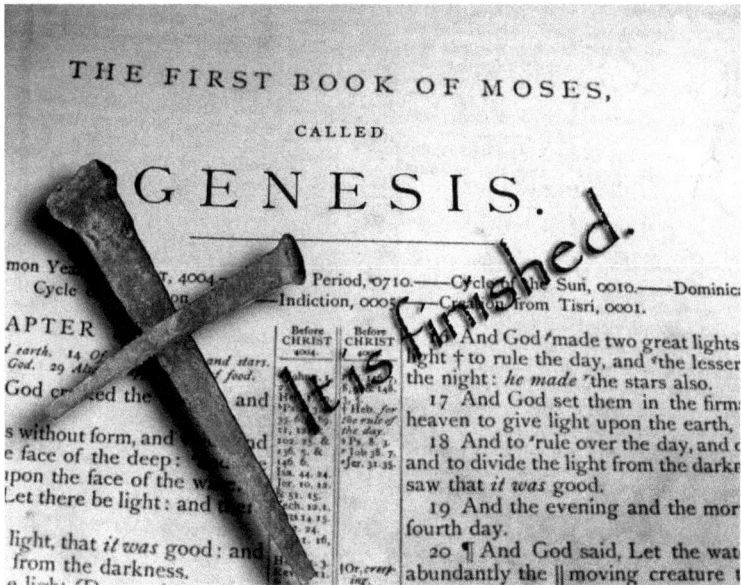

We shall proceed to analyze a doctrine that **has caused great confusion** within the Christian world, and furthermore, many souls have not come to Christ and received the grace of God because of this foundational premise in theology. We shall speak of what has been accepted as the **"Doctrine of Original Sin"** in Christianity.

The Bible teaches us in the book of Romans:

"Wherefore, **as by one man sin entered into the world,** and death by sin; and so death passed upon all men, for that all have sinned"

"For if by one man's offense death reigned by one; much more they which receive abundance of grace and of the gift of righteousness **shall reign in life by one,** Jesus Christ.)"

"Therefore, as by the offense of one *judgment came* upon all men to condemnation; even so **by the righteousness of one** *the free gift came* **upon all men unto justification of life."**

"For as by one man's disobedience many were made sinners, so by the obedience of one shall many be made righteous."

(ROMANS 5: 12, 17-19)

It is interesting to note that **within the same chapter** that the principal sense of the doctrine of original sin is found (v.12) the Bible states that on the merit of Christ, the justification for life is available to all humanity (v.18), as long as grace and forgiveness are chosen.

"And the Spirit and the bride say, Come. And let him that heareth say, Come. And let him that is athirst come. And whosoever will, let him take the water of life freely." (Revelation 22: 17)

Those who teach the doctrine of the original sin give to understand (perhaps without knowing it), that the **sin** of Adam is more powerful that the **triumph** of Christ

We have been taught that by the sin of Adam, the human race was contaminated, and we are born with this blemish of sin. Nevertheless, the Bible declares **that Jesus removed all the effects of sin** that weighed on humanity **through Adam**.

> "Christ hath redeemed us from the curse of the law, being made a curse for us: for it is written, Cursed is everyone that hangeth on a tree." (Gal 3:13)

The Word also says:

> "And you, being dead in your sins and the uncircumcision of your flesh, hath he **quickened together** with him, having forgiven you all trespasses;
> **Blotting out** the handwriting of ordinances that was against us, which was contrary to us, and took it out of the way, nailing it to his cross; *And* having spoiled principalities and powers, he made a show of them openly, triumphing over them in it." Col 2: 13-15

Those who teach the doctrine of the original sin give to understand (perhaps without knowing it), that the sin of Adam is more powerful that the triumph of Christ

HOW DID IT ALL BEGIN?

Let us examine a period of history, as reliable sources recount:

- "It was universally believed that man was created in the image of God, pure and holy, and the fall was his own fault. The magnitude of man's sin and the dire consequences were not fully debated before the controversy between Pelagius and Augustine in the Fifth century." (Source: Phillip SCAF. The history of the Christian Church, Vol.11 P. 246)

- "Throughout man's history, the theology of depravity has been attributed to Adam. Augustine, (354-430 AD) who is credited with the concept of original sin, submitted that the fall of Adam corrupted humanity, transforming the human race into a mass of sin. All men inherit both traits: the pull of sin and the guilt, because in Adam's sin all humanity has sinned." (Source: ISBE, 1979)

- "Pelagius (370-440 AD) rejecting the argument of those that insisted human frailty was the reason for their sin, made the point that God created all human beings free to choose between good and bad; and sin is a voluntary choice. Celestius, a disciple of Pelagius, rejected the church doctrine of original sin and the necessity of infant baptism.

- He (Pelagius) blamed the moral laxity in Rome for the doctrine of "divine grace" (as taught by Augustine). He attacked this teaching in all the territories where moral law was in jeopardy. He reasoned that if one were not responsible for his good or bad actions, no one would refrain themselves from indulging in sin. Pelagius soon had a considerable amount of followers in Rome." (Source: Britannica 1979 VII, Page 837-8).

WHEN WE ANALYZE THE SCRIPTURES, WE DISCOVER:

- Adam and Eve were created in a state of innocence and **were good** (Gen.1:27,31)

- The Word of God teaches us that there is a time in a person's life, when they have no understanding and cannot discern between good and evil (Deut. 1:39) and they cannot **reject evil and choose good** (Isaiah 7:15-16)

- When sin is committed there is a separation between God and the person who chose to sin (Isaiah 59:1-2)

- God has made clear that the spiritual consequences that sin brings fall completely on the person committing the act of sin. He says:

"the soul that sinneth, it shall die" (Ezekiel 18: 2-4,20)

- Jesus used the children as an example of humility (Matt 18: 2-4)

- Jesus also said the kingdom of heaven is made up of children (Mark 10: 14-15)

- The Apostle Paul used children as a model of purity (1 Corin. 14:20)

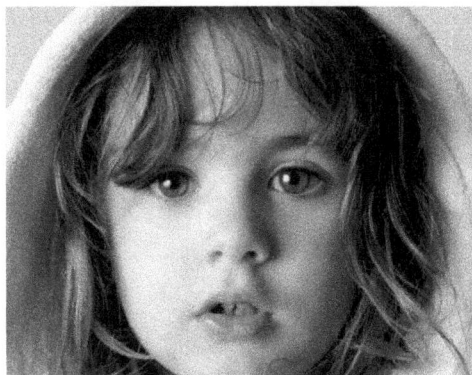

- God will judge each one according to the harsh words they have spoken and their individual actions (Matthew 12:36-37; Romans 2:6; 2 Corin. 5:10; Rev.20: 12-15)

- Jesus Christ paid the price required by God to remove the sin of Adam (Rom.5: 15-21; Hebrews 9). He is the second Adam (1 Corin.15:45-49) who came from heaven to restore what the first Adam had lost (Matt. 18:11), and He redeemed us from the curse (Galatians 3:13)

It is a fact that neither Jesus nor the first Christians believed or taught that newborn babes entered this world already sinners and deserving hell; but this same doctrine was introduced in the **fifth century** of this era; therefore, we should believe and understand that the preceding Biblical verses are showing us:

"The whole human race is **born** in a state of **innocence**, the same as Adam in the Garden of Eden (signifying that **no child who dies is destined for hell, but goes to heaven**);

And when someone, after being able to discern good and evil, exercising their free will decides to disobey God and is corrupted, suffers a spiritual death until he/she repents and receives, also voluntarily, grace for forgiveness and is justified by God through Jesus Christ."

The case of King David

In reading Psalm 51, we may be predisposed to believe that David sinned before being born (or conceived); but as we further examine the circumstance he speaks directly of, a more perfect understanding is achieved.

David said:

> "Behold, I was shapen in iniquity; and in sin did my mother conceive me." (Psalm 51:5)

We will see that David was referring to a sin of his mother and not any sin that he had committed for being born.

Let us examine some key verses:

1Samuel 12:12

"And when ye saw that **Nahash** the king of the children of Ammon came against you, ye said unto me, Nay; but a king shall reign over us: when the LORD your God *was* your king"

2Samuel 17:25

"And Absalom made Amasa captain of the host instead of Joab: which Amasa *was* a man's son, whose name *was* Ithra an Israelite, that went in to **Abigail the daughter of Nahash, sister to Zeruiah** Joab's mother"

In these previous verses, the Bible tells us that the king **Nahash** ammonite had two daughters called **Abigail** and **Sarvia**.

Now, let us read these verses:

1Chron. 2: 13-17

> **"And Jesse begot** his firstborn Eliab, and Abinadab the second, and Shimma the third, Nethaneel the fourth, Raddai the fifth, Ozem the sixth, **David** the seventh:
>
> Whose **sisters *were* Zeruiah, and Abigail**. And the sons of Zeruiah; Abishai, and Joab, and Asahel, three. And Abigail bore Amasa: and the father of Amasa *was* Jether the Ishmaelite."

Those verses state that **David's mother was the woman of King Nahash** and committed adultery with Jesse.

David was referring to a sin of his mother

The fruit of this relationship was David.

It is clear now why Jesse did not present David to Samuel (1Sam 16:1-13) when the prophet went to his home to anoint one of his sons as future king of Israel:

> "And Samuel said unto Jesse, Are here all thy children? And he said, There remaineth yet the youngest, and, behold, he keepeth the sheep.

And Samuel said unto Jesse, Send and fetch him: for we will not sit down till he come hither." (1Sam 16:11)

It is also clear now, the cause of why his brothers despised him:

"And Eliab his eldest brother heard when he spake unto the men; and Eliab's anger was kindled against David, and he said, Why camest thou down hither? and with whom hast thou left those few sheep in the wilderness? I know thy pride, and the naughtiness of thine heart; for thou art come down that thou mightest see the battle." (1 Sam.17:28)

In addition, we can understand better, why David did not name to any of his brothers as head of his army, but the sons of his sisters and why king Nahash had a special esteem for David and "had shown him mercy"

"Now it came to pass after this, that Nahash the king of the children of Ammon died, and his son reigned in his stead.

And David said, I will shew kindness unto Hanun the son of Nahash, because his father shewed kindness to me. And David sent messengers to comfort him concerning his father. So the servants of David came into the land of the children of Ammon to Hanun, to comfort him."

1Chronicles 19: 1-2

The Lord Jesus tells us:

"Search the Scriptures" (John 5:39)…

…And this is precisely what we shall do in this book

Let us go deeper into the waters of Biblical revelation where we shall discover some of the details of God actions that normally are far from man's knowledge.

Let us come to analyze the **grace** of God and the **salvation** with a totally Biblical approach, but distinct to what we are used to hear

Salvation: The story that is continually written

If there is an important theme we may trace through the Bible from the fall of man by disobedience, it is the story of salvation.

We see that before banishing Adam and Eve from paradise, God gave them the promise of redemption when He told the serpent *(Satan, also Rev.12:29 and Ezek 28:13)* that the seed of woman would bruise his head.

It was also prophesized that a child would be born of a virgin:

"Therefore the Lord himself shall give you a sign; Behold, a virgin shall conceive, and bear a son, and shall call his name Immanuel." (This means "God with us") (Isaiah 7:14)

Isaiah also tells us that the child shall be a prince and shall be acknowledged in an extraordinary manner:

> "For unto us a child is born, unto us a son is given: and the government shall be upon his shoulder: and his name shall be called Wonderful, Counselor, The mighty God, The everlasting Father, The Prince of peace."
> (Isaiah 9:6)

The Bible declares that Jesus was born of a virgin woman; **Mary**, the blessed of God and among all woman by the declaration of faith made to the angel Gabriel (Luke 1:28)

Jesus was born, grew, and fulfilled all the purpose of His coming to this world: To **Redeem** all humanity and **Restore** all things.

Apostle Peter wrote on one occasion:

> "This is the stone which was set at naught of you builders, which is become the head of the corner.
> Neither is there salvation in any other: for **there is none other name** under heaven given among men, whereby we must be saved"
> (ACTS 4:11-12)

On another occasion, the Apostle Paul declares:

> "… that is, the word of faith, which we preach;
> That if thou shalt confess with thy mouth the Lord Jesus, and shalt believe in thine heart that God hath raised him from the dead, thou shalt be saved…
> **For whosoever shall call upon the name of the Lord shall be saved.** (ROMANS 10: 8B-13)

The same Jesus said:

> "For God so loved the world, that he gave his only begotten Son, **that whosoever believeth in him** should not perish, but have everlasting life.
> For God sent not his Son into the world to condemn the world; but that the world through him might be saved." (John 3:16-17)

"For I came down from heaven, not to do mine own will, but the will of him that sent me.

And **this is the Father's will** which hath sent me, that of all which he hath given me I should lose nothing, but should raise it up again at the last day.

"And this is the will of him that sent me, that every one which seeth the Son, and believeth on him, may have everlasting life: and I will raise him up at the last day." (John 6:38-40)

"And if any man hear my words, and believe not, I judge him not: for I came not to judge the world, **but to save** the world." (John 12:47)

We should take note there is a great revelation in these words.

They all speak of the salvation offered to **all** human beings who would believe on the name of Jesus and would acknowledge Him as Lord. A person's race or social standing is irrelevant, although it was not always this way.

There was a time when the promises of God were for one people exclusively: The Jews. To better understand why God did this, let us read the biblical narrative.

> They all speak of the salvation offered to **all** human beings who would believe on the name of Jesus and would acknowledge Him as Lord

Brief historical analysis

A brief historical analysis of the Biblical Timeline:

In the creation, God placed Adam in Eden or Paradise; then created a woman as a companion and married them (Gen.2:7, 8, 15, 18, 21-25)

He then **blessed them** (Gen.1:28) by pure grace and love, as God had created them so they may have communion with Him.

When the man disobeyed God's commandment, man was cursed, along with the earth and the serpent (Gen.3:3-17)

Men then became so corrupt that God repented of having created man on the earth (Gen.6:6) and decided to destroy all on the earth: man, beast, and reptiles, fowl…! All!

Nevertheless, we read that although he was surrounded by such a sinful society, there was a man who found grace before the eyes of God (Gen 6:8) as he loved God, sought Him and desired to please Him.
His name was Noah.

God made a pact with Noah (Gen. 6:18; (:9) **and passed him the blessing** (Gen. 9:1) that he had before given to Adam and Eve.

However, in the second blessing that God gave to the humanity through Noah, He did not give back **the dominion** usurped by Satan to Adam (compare Gen. 1:28 to Gen. 9:1)

God is Righteous

This is why in the desert, when addressing Christ concerning this dominion (Luke 4:5-6), the Lord did not accuse him as stating a lie but acknowledged, shamefully, that such dominion Satan had was valid.

In spite of this, the Bible declares that afterwards, **when Jesus Christ died on the cross, all the authority Satan had was taken by Christ** (Col 2:15; Rev. 5:5) and is **now shared with the Church**. (Eph. 1:19-23; 2:6; 3:10-12)

Firmness rewards you.

God is Righteous; and **it is worth choosing to live without allowing oneself to be dragged through the mud by the currents of this world**. That person who will live righteously will be rewarded. God will honor his faith and obedience. Noah is a living and real example.

The Bible states in the book of 2Chronicles that:

> "For the eyes of the Lord run to and fro throughout the whole earth, to show himself strong in the behalf of them whose heart is perfect toward him." (2 Chron.16:9)

Due to the manner in which Noah chose to live, humanity and all species of animals and fowl were not extinguished.

Let us take note of the blessing Noah obtained **by obeying** all that God had told him (Gen.6:22), and then passed to his son **Shem** (Gen. 9:26).

The blessing was passed from one generation to the next generation (Gen.11:10-31) and much later the moment arrived when God decided to separate unto Him a holy people, set apart from unrighteousness.

The Bible relates that **Abram**, son of Terah, descendant of Shem, was called by God and instructed to leave the land of his fathers and go to a place He would show him; and God would bless him.

We see that now the blessing of God would take on further significance:

God decided to raise a people that would have his blessing and chose Abram (whose name He later changed to Abraham, which means "father of a multitude" (Gen. 17:1-5) and he would be the patriarch of this blessed people (whom we now recognize as Jews).

A very interesting situation:

We have an interesting point here: God had spoken directly to Abraham and promised him great blessings (Gen.12:1-4), if Abraham obeyed... and Abraham responded by obeying. (The Bible states that through Abraham's obedience, his faith was counted for righteousness (Romans 4:3; Heb 11:8);

Nevertheless, God had to test the faith of Abraham in a peculiar manner; **and it was not until Abraham obeyed** and passed the test, that God swore to him with an oath that he would receive the blessing as promised. (Gen.22: 1-18; Heb.11:17-19).

In our days, we have been blessed further as a result of Jesus Christ's perfect obedience in life.

"Who, being in the form of God, but made himself of no reputation, and took upon him the form of a servant, and was made in the likeness of men:"

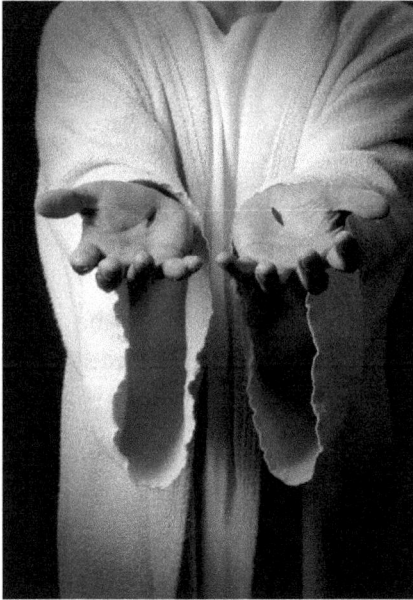

"And being found in fashion as a man, he humbled himself, and **became obedient unto death,** even the death of the cross." (Philippians 2: 5-8); And who "spoiled principalities and powers, he made a show of them openly, **triumphing over them** in it" (Colossians 2:15)

God has extended his blessing that it may cover all humanity (without regard to race or nation), so that they may receive His grace and forgiveness for sin on the merits of the Lord Jesus Christ.

This is what the Bible says:

"*That* was the true Light, which lighteth every man that cometh into the world... **But as many as received him, to them gave he power to become the sons of God...**
(John 1:9-12)

"Therefore **it is of faith**, that it might be by grace; to the end the promise might be sure to all the seed; not to that only which is of the law, but to that also which is of the faith of Abraham; who is the father of us all

And therefore it was imputed to him for righteousness

Who was delivered for our offenses, and was raised again for our justification." (Romans 4:16, 22, 25)

"... But now in Christ Jesus ye who sometimes were far off are made nigh by the blood of Christ..."

"... And came and preached peace to you which were afar off, and to them that were nigh."

"For <u>through him we both have access by one Spirit unto the Father</u>..." (Ephesians 2:11-22)

We see that the Bible declares that:
"Therefore by the offense of one judgment came upon all men to condemnation, even **so by the righteousness of one the free gift came upon all men unto justification of life**"   (Romans 5:18)

We ask then,

Does this mean that the entire world is now automatically justified before God?

The answer is NO; but **everyone in the world has the opportunity** of being justified, as the Apostle Peter said:

"The Lord is not slack concerning his promise, as some men count slackness; but is longsuffering to us-ward, not willing that any should perish, but that all should come to repentance."
(2 Peter 3:9)

WHAT IS, THEN, THE FULLNESS OF THIS **SALVATION?**

Firstly, let us recall the words of our Lord Jesus:

> "… But <u>he</u> that **shall endure unto the end, the same shall be saved."**
> (Matt 24: 11-13)

Peter also wrote:

"… That the trial of your faith… might be found unto praise and honor and glory at the appearing of Jesus Christ… **Receiving the end of your faith,** *even* **the salvation of** *your* **souls**."   (1 Peter 1: 6-9)

This is how we see it in the book of Hebrews:

> "Take heed, brethren, lest there be in any of you an evil heart of unbelief, in departing from the living God. But exhort one another daily, while it is called Today; lest any of you be hardened through the deceitfulness of sin. For we are made partakers of Christ, **if we hold the beginning of our confidence steadfast unto the end**" (Hebrews 3: 12-14)

The best way I can use to **explain salvation** is to compare it to an IMMIGRANT VISA that allows a particular person to enter and live in a country, and then apply for citizenship.

There are **requirements** that must be satisfied for them to obtain the VISA (and in acquiring it, the person then has a **privilege**); and in addition, **there are norms that must be respected and obeyed in order to not lose this privilege.**

The Bible demonstrates we all have access to the Father by one Spirit and we are part of His family, people, and kingdom (Ephesians 2:18); nevertheless, before coming to Christ we were sinful and malicious.

> "That at that time ye were without Christ, being aliens from the commonwealth of Israel, and strangers from the covenants of promise, having no hope, and without God in the world" (Ephesians 2:12)

The Word has more to say of our **manner of life before**:

"But evil men and seducers shall wax worse and worse, deceiving, and being deceived" (2Tim 3:13}

"Being filled with all unrighteousness, fornication, wickedness, covetousness, maliciousness; full of envy, murder, debate, deceit, malignity; whisperers, Backbiters, haters of God, despiteful, proud, boasters, inventors of evil things, disobedient to parents, Without understanding, covenant breakers, without natural affection, implacable, unmerciful." (Romans 1:29-31)

An excellent manner to explain salvation is to compare it to an IMMIGRANT VISA

The following chart demonstrates the weight of sin on our soul:

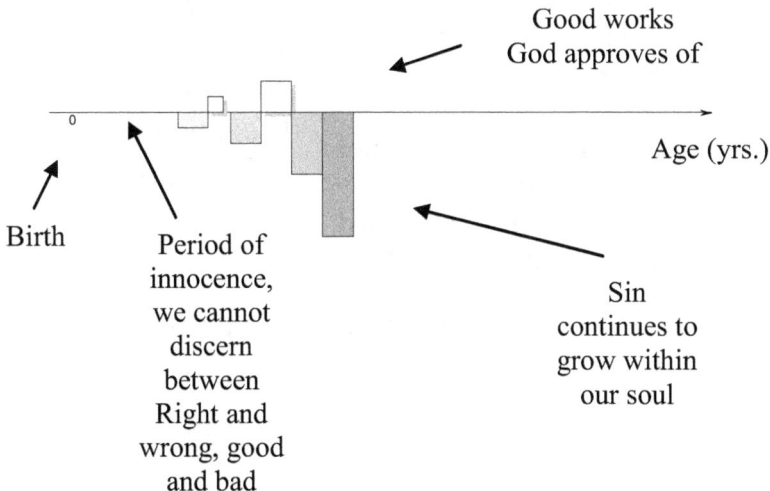

Good works
God approves of

0

Age (yrs.)

Birth

Period of innocence, we cannot discern between Right and wrong, good and bad

Sin continues to grow within our soul

The Bible says **all humanity** shall **give account** to God on that final judgment day:

"And I saw a great white throne, and him that sat on it, from whose face the earth and the heaven fled away...

And I saw the dead, small and great, stand before God; and the books were opened: and another book was opened, which is *the book* of life: and **the dead were judged** out of those things which were **written** in the books, **according to their works...**

And **whosoever was not found written in** the book of life was cast into the lake of fire."

Some will have their names written in the book of life; and others will not.

(Revelations 20: 11-15)

The Bible says all the world will be judged (Christian and non- Christian); the difference being some will be found without **fault or sin**, as the blood of the Lamb (Jesus Christ) erased all their sins, and others shall be judged according to their works and the **dictates of their conscience**.

As Apostle Paul declares in the letter to the Romans:

"For there is no respect of persons with God.
For as many as have sinned without law shall also perish without law: and as many as have sinned in the law shall be judged by the law;
For not the hearers of the law *are* just before God, but the doers of the law shall be justified.

For when the Gentiles, which have not the law, do by nature the things contained in the law, these, having not the law, are a law unto themselves:
Which show the work of the law written in their hearts, their conscience also bearing witness, and *their* **thoughts the mean while accusing or else excusing** one another;) In the day when God shall judge the secrets of men by Jesus Christ according to my gospel." (Romans 2: 11-16)

The Missing Link in Theology

Where the hope does finishes?

Let us return to the **first question** posed at the beginning of the book:

> Is there hope for someone to have their name written in the book of life on the final judgment day; God willing, and spend eternity in heaven?

The instinctive reply from those of us educated as Christians would be NO, that if someone dies without Christ he is condemned of God to hell and will go to the last judgment to be re-condemned and sent to the lake of fire.

The Bible states emphatically that God is a just judge. **No one is condemned at a hearing without a clear demonstration of guilt**. There will be those who have rejected Christ and others who never had the opportunity to hear the good news of salvation.

Jesus said:

> "For God sent not his Son into the world to condemn the world; but that the world through him might be saved.
>
> He that believeth on him is not condemned: but **he that believeth not is condemned already**, because he hath not believed in the name of the only begotten Son of God.
>
> And <u>this is the condemnation</u>, that light is come into the world, and <u>men loved darkness rather than light</u>, because their deeds were evil.
>
> For every one that doeth evil hateth the light, neither cometh to the light, lest his deeds should be reproved. (John 3:17-20)

Talking about whipping

He also said:

"And that servant, which knew his lord's will, and prepared not himself, neither did according to his will, shall be beaten with many stripes.

But **he that knew not, and did commit things worthy of stripes, shall be beaten with few stripes**. For unto whomsoever much is given, of him shall be much required: and to whom men have committed much, of him they will ask the more."

(Luke 12:47-48)

In elaborating, **when someone dies without having heard of Christ** (the gospel message must be explained correctly), this person **never had** the opportunity **to accept or reject** the grace of God, and will be judged according to his/her works at the final judgment.

The fact he did not go to heaven at the hour of death can be considered **"few stripes"** and God may determine that at the final day that soul may be accepted into heaven or rejected and cast into the lake of fire. (Revelations 20:12-15)

Then the natural question that would follow is:

Where do those who receive "few stripes" go, while they await final judgment?

In answer to this question, let us analyze the history of two men spoken by our Lord:

"There was a certain rich man, which was clothed in purple and fine linen, and fared sumptuously every day:

And there was a certain beggar named Lazarus, which was laid at his gate, full of sores,

And desiring to be fed with the crumbs which fell from the rich man's table: moreover the dogs came and licked his sores.

"And it came to pass, that the beggar died, and was carried by the angels into **Abraham's bosom**: the rich man also died, and was buried;"

"And in **hell** he lifted up his eyes, being in torments, and seeth Abraham afar off, and Lazarus in his bosom.
And he cried and said, Father Abraham, have mercy on me, and send Lazarus, that he may dip the tip of his finger in water, and cool my tongue; for I am tormented in this flame.

But Abraham said, Son, remember that thou in thy lifetime receivedst thy good things, and likewise Lazarus evil things: but now he is comforted, and thou art tormented.

And beside all this, between us and you there is **a great gulf fixed**: so that they which would pass from hence to you cannot; neither can they pass to us, that would come from thence."

(Luke 16: 19-26)

"Abraham's Bosom" is a place.

As I comprehend, and considering that Jesus refers to "Abraham's bosom" as if an actual **LOCATION** and not a "temporary state of being", I believe God has established this same place, although not with those who had gone to paradise (Ephe. 4:8-10);

But those judged unworthy in the tribunal of Christ (principally those with the characteristics expressed in the **second question** presented at the outset).

I firmly believe the Bible teaches us that someone who has lived a "Christian" life, (believed that Jesus died on the cross for him or her), goes directly to the **tribunal of Christ** on expiring.

There they are judged, as the Word states:

> "Wherefore we labor, that, whether present or absent, we may be accepted of him.
> For we must all appear before the judgment seat of Christ; that every one may receive the things

done in his body, according to that he hath done, **whether it be good or bad.**" (2 Corin. 5: 9-10)

As a result of this judgment, each person is sent to one of three places:

> o Heaven
> o Hades; or
> o Abraham's bosom

To those who go to **heaven** it shall be told:

"Come ye blessed of my Father, inherit the kingdom prepared for you from the foundation of the world." (Matt: 25:34)

"Well done, thou good and faithful servant: thou hast been faithful over a few things, I will make thee ruler over many things: enter thou into the joy of thy lord." (Matt 25: 21)

To those who go to **Hades** it shall be told:

"I never knew you; depart from me, ye that work iniquity" (Matt 7:23)

"Depart from me, ye cursed, into everlasting fire, prepared for the devil and his angels" (Matt 25:41)

Those who go to **Abraham's bosom** shall suffer **anguish in being separated from the Lord**, until the final judgment day when they are called by God to heaven; and are not condemned:

> "For if we judge ourselves, we should not be judged; But when we are judged we are chastened of the Lord, **that we should not be condemned with the world**" (1Corin. 11:31-32)

On the other hand, those who **die without having put their faith in the Lord Jesus Christ** will go directly to **Hades** and will wait there until the final day of Judgment.

It is among these that after being **judged according to their works** as their **conscience** had dictated to them, God may condemn them to the lake of fire or have their name written in the book of life so they may enter heaven and spend eternity there.

Those saved from here **will not be rewarded** as faithful Christians when they stand before the Lord.

In this we now understand that as there exists a possibility your name may be erased from the book of life (Rev.3:5; 22:19); the possibility of adding your name to the book of life is also real; at the final hour of judgment.

Those who die without having put their faith in the Lord Jesus Christ will go directly to Hades and will wait there until the final day of Judgment

Let us consider these words of the Lord Jesus:

> "If I had not come and spoken unto them, they **had not had sin**: but now they have no cloak for their sin." (John 15:22)

> "And some of the Pharisees which were with him heard these words and said unto him, Are we blind also?

> Jesus said unto them, If **ye were blind, ye should have no sin**: but now ye say, We see; therefore your sin remaineth." (John 9:40-41)

The Lord's words are spiritual.

He spoke of **spiritual blindness** and its relation to being guilty of sin.

Let us bear in mind that God knows our hearts

> "**The heart** is deceitful above all things, and desperately wicked: who can know it?

> I the LORD search the heart, I try the reins, even to give every man **according to his ways**, and according to the fruit of his doings." (Jeremiah 17:9-10)

As we see, with respect to what happens to all people on the final day, God has the last word, as He only is Judge.

God had said beforehand, **He desires not the death of sinner**, but that he would repent:

> "… Say unto them, As I live, saith the Lord GOD, <u>I have no pleasure in the death of the wicked</u>; **but that the wicked turn from his way and live:** turn ye, turn ye from your evil ways; for why will ye die, O house of Israel?"
> (Ezekiel 33:10-11)

> "The Lord is not slack concerning his promise, as some men count slackness; but is **longsuffering** to us-ward, <u>not willing that any should perish</u>, but that all should come to repentance. " (2Peter 3:9)

We should remember the Bible says that sin brings forth death; not only sins we consider "big":

"If ye fulfill the royal law according to the Scripture, Thou shalt love thy neighbor as thyself, ye do well:

We find that God will punish believers in judgment, to avoid condemning them with sinners on the final judgment day

But **if ye have respect to persons, ye commit sin, and are convinced of the law as transgressors**.

For whosoever shall keep the whole law, and yet offend in one point, **he is guilty of all**.

For he that said, Do not commit adultery, said also, Do not kill. Now if thou commit no adultery, yet if thou kill, thou art become a **transgressor of the law**.

So speak ye, and so do, as they that shall be judged by the law of liberty.

For he shall have judgment without mercy, that hath showed no mercy; **and mercy rejoiceth against judgment**." (James 2: 8-13)

Another interesting Scripture Portion:

"… For if we would judge ourselves, we should not be judged.

But **when we are judged, we are chastened of the Lord, that we should not be condemned** with the world."
(1 Corin.11:27-32)

"For whom the Lord loveth he <u>chasteneth, and scourgeth</u> every son whom he receiveth…
(Hebrews 12:6-8)

We find that God will punish believers in judgment, to avoid condemning them with sinners on the final judgment day.

Even a premature death due to sin, is a judgment of God in order to avoid eternal damnation.

When a person repents of all his sins, he will ask forgiveness of God and put his faith in Christ Jesus.

The Bible says: "Wash you, make you clean; put away the evil of your doings from before mine eyes; cease to do evil;
> Learn to do well; seek judgment, relieve the oppressed, judge the fatherless, plead for the widow.

> **Come now, and let us reason together**, saith the LORD: though your sins be as scarlet, they shall be as white as snow; though they be red like crimson, they shall be as wool."
> (Isaiah 1:16-18)

"… the blood of Jesus Christ his Son cleanseth us from all sin. If we confess our sins, he is faithful and just to forgive us our sins, and to cleanse us from all unrighteousness."
(1 John 1: 7, 9)

The following graphically illustrates what becomes of our sin, after we receive forgiveness through faith in Christ:

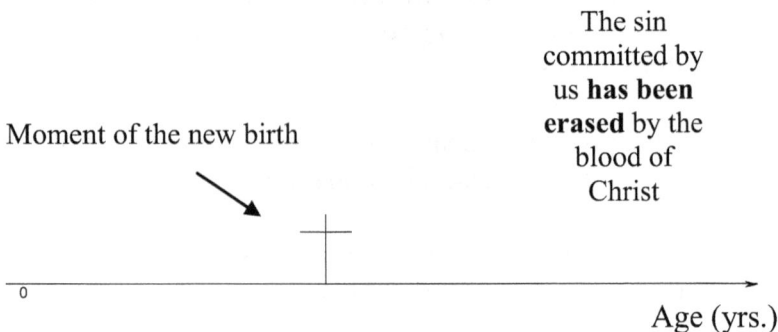

Moment of the new birth

The sin committed by us **has been erased** by the blood of Christ

0

Age (yrs.)

It is said then that in coming to God and asking forgiveness for our sins we recognize the evil we have committed, and have the attitude of repentance and rejection of our sins.

The Bible tells us that **God causes us to be born again by the Spirit**, and all things are made new:

> "… Jesus answered, Verily, verily, I say unto thee, Except a man be born of water and of the Spirit, he cannot enter into the kingdom of God.
> That which is born of the flesh is flesh; and that which is born of the Spirit is spirit.
> Marvel not that I said unto thee, Ye must be born again…"   (John 3: 3-8)

WE HAVE THE CHANCE TO START ANEW.

But now with a great advantage:

- We now **have the Holy Spirit** living in us and He shall **teach** us to live correctly, as God wills
- The Holy Spirit will **convict** us of sin and exhort us to immediately repent on committing any sinful act, after we have been initially purified of past sin; and,

- **Past** sin that had power over us **no longer** can dominate us.

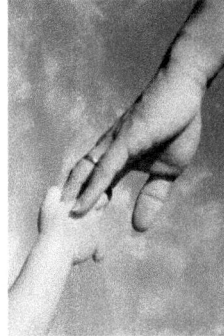

The Holy Word Declares:

"Howbeit when he, the Spirit of truth, is come, he will guide you into all truth..." (John 16:13)

"Being confident of this very thing, that he which hath begun a good work in you will **perform** it until the day of Jesus Christ" (Phil. 1:6)

"**Let not sin** therefore **reign** in your mortal body, that ye should obey it in the lusts thereof.
Neither yield ye your members as instruments of unrighteousness unto sin: but yield yourselves unto God, as those that are alive from the dead, and your members as instruments of righteousness unto God.

For sin shall not have dominion over you: for ye are not under the law, but under grace."
(Romans 6:12-14)

And, **What about the Future sins?**

A common error in interpreting Scripture is a belief that all our **FUTURE** sins are instantly forgiven when we receive Christ as our personal Savior. Those with this belief put forth that when Christ died for us on the cross of Calvary; all our sins were still in the future and were paid for.

This is an **immature** understanding of God and his pact with humanity, as

The Holy Spirit will convict us of sin and exhort us to immediately repent on committing any sinful act

He declares in His Word that He is not mocked:

"Be not deceived; God is not mocked: for whatsoever a man soweth, that shall he also reap. For **he that soweth to his flesh shall of the flesh reap corruption**; but he that soweth to the Spirit shall of the Spirit reap life everlasting." (Galatians 6:7-8)

What the Bible does say is:

"But now the righteousness of God without the law is manifested, being witnessed by the law and the prophets;

Even the **righteousness of God which is by faith of Jesus Christ** unto all and upon all them that believe: for there is no difference:

For all have sinned, and come short of the glory of God;

Being justified freely by his grace through the redemption that is in Christ Jesus:

Whom God hath set forth to be a propitiation through **faith in his blood**, to declare his righteousness for the remission of **sins that are past**, through the forbearance of God;

To declare, I say, at this time his righteousness: that he might be just, and the justifier of him which believeth in Jesus." (Romans 3:21-26)

"But he that lacketh these things is blind, and cannot see afar off, and hath forgotten that he was purged from his **old sins**." (2 Peter 1:9)

What then occurs when a Christian sins after receiving the grace of God in his life?

The Bible says:

> "…If we confess our sins, He is faithful and just to forgive us our sins, and to cleanse us from all unrighteousness"…

> "The blood of Jesus Christ His son cleanseth us from all sin…" (1John 1:9, 7)

To further explain, if we do commit an act of sin (and there is none who will not, as we are not perfect but are perfected), our soul has the **blemish** of this sin; but on recognizing and repenting of it, we ask forgiveness of God, and IIe forgives and washes us, maintaining us pure before Him.

We should continually examine ourselves in our daily walk (**examine yourself with care**, Paul told young Timothy); and avoid all rebellion in our behavior towards the Holy Spirit by all means.

> "Wherefore gird up the loins of your mind, be sober, and hope to the end for the grace that is to be brought unto you at the revelation of Jesus Christ;
>
> As obedient children, **not fashioning yourselves according to the former lusts** in your ignorance:

If we do commit an act of sin, our soul has the blemish of this sin

But as he which hath called you is holy, so be ye
holy in all manner of conversation;

Because it is written, Be ye holy; for I am holy.
And if ye call on the Father, who **without respect of
persons judgeth according to every man's work**,
pass the time of your sojourning here in fear:"
(1 Peter 1:13-17)

The Bible clearly establishes that **Christians will sin** in
this life; and forgiveness through Christ is there only
resource:

"If we say we have no sin, we deceive
ourselves, and the truth is not in us" (1 John 1:8)

The Unnatural Procedure.

Subsequently, we will say that it is **unnatural** for a true Christian to continue a life of sin.

There is no habitual sin.

This is what the Word has to say:

> "He that **practices** sin is of the devil; for from the beginning the devil sins. To this end the Son of God has been manifested, that he might undo the works of the devil.
>
> Whoever has been begotten of God **does not practice** sin, because his seed abides in him, and

he cannot sin, because he has been begotten of God." (1 John 3:8-9) *(1889 Darby Bible)*

Whosoever is born of God does not practice sin; to reiterate, does not sin habitually. There is not a continual practice of sin as the sons of perdition do.

The true Christian puts off sin and grows spiritually, knowing that all practice of sin affects their faith negatively and imperils their soul.

Now, based on what the Word says:

> "Follow peace with all men, and holiness, without which no man shall see the Lord:" (Hebrews 12:14)

> "… As obedient children, not fashioning yourselves according to the former lusts in your ignorance:
> But as he which hath called you is holy, so be ye holy in all manner of conversation;
> Because it is written, Be ye holy; for I am holy."
> (1 Peter 1: 13-16)

We should then answer the following question:

Will a Christian who commits sin enter heaven?

Many believers say that "if we sin we cannot be saved". Nevertheless, we consider that pride, jealousy, and bitterness are common failures. No one suggests that those who fall into these sins are lost. Even further, if it is insisted by some that God presently demands perfection in believers, then we pose the next question:

> "Is a Christian rooted in Christ based on **their** righteousness, or is the righteousness **of Christ** attributed to them by faith?"

> If a Christian is saved by living a life without sin, then salvation is no longer by grace, but by works!

Consequentially, if a believer is only accepted having no faults, then the Christian is not free from condemnation as insisted by Paul in Romans 8:1.

The beleiver then enter a continual exercise of fear followed by condemnation as we examine our soul; thus not entering into the joy of the knowledge that we are saved.

The Bible tells us:

> "But God commendeth his love toward us, in that, while we were yet sinners, Christ died for us.
> Much more then, **being now justified by his blood, we shall be saved from wrath through him**.

> For if, when we were enemies, we were reconciled to God by the death of his Son, **much more, being reconciled, we shall be saved by his life**..." (Romans 5:8-11)

Also:

> "For in that he himself hath suffered being tempted, he is able to **succor** them that are tempted." (Hebrews 2:18)

> "Now unto him that **is able to keep you from falling**, and to present you faultless before the presence of his glory with exceeding joy, To the only wise God our Savior, be glory and majesty, dominion and power, both now and ever. Amen." (Jude 24-25)

It is so clear that the "God that so loved us to provide for our salvation, also loves us enough to keep us saved all the way to glory".

This conviction maintains our joy in Him.

As we also are conscious of **our existence in a depraved world,** we should be encouraged in knowing we can continually ask the Holy Spirit to **examine** our heart; and if He reveals unconfessed sin, we then can confess our sin and repent.

Remember the Lord Jesus, as He taught us to pray (the Lord's Prayer), tells us that every day, as well as asking for our

> It is so clear that the "God that so loved us to provide for our salvation, also loves us enough to keep us saved all the way to glory".

daily bread, we should ask God to forgive us for all our trespasses.

The Lord Jesus is Faithful, always Faithful. **He will never abandon us** to the enemy at the end of our life.

The Bible says:

> "… God is faithful, who will not suffer you to be tempted above that ye are able; but will with the temptation also make a way to escape, that ye may be able to bear it."
> (1 Corin. 10:13)

> "If we believe not, yet he abideth faithful: he cannot deny himself (2 Timothy 2:13)

The Word also teaches us that those in Christ "have crucified the flesh with its passions and desires" and **should walk in the SPIRIT"** (Galatians 5:24-25);
And in being lead by the Spirit of God we have the testimony that we are the **children of God** (Romans 8:14)

> For that person who walks **in obedience** to God, being **sensitive** to the leading of the **Holy Spirit**, watching in order to keep from falling into the wiles of the Deceiver;
>
> **Working on the weak areas** the Spirit reveals exist and allowing Him to **mold** and transform them from

glory to glory in the image of Christ Jesus every day (2 Corin.3:18);

Putting aside their personal agenda and permitting **the will of God** to be done in their life (Psalm 138:8; Matt 6:10; 26:39); they will grow and mature spiritually every day.

Such a person would **have learned** to defend themselves from the attacks and temptations, and would experience the victorious power of the cross in various manifestations as they walk with Christ; as also they will be able to say as did Apostle Paul: **"Yet not I, but Christ liveth in me"** (Galatians:2:20)

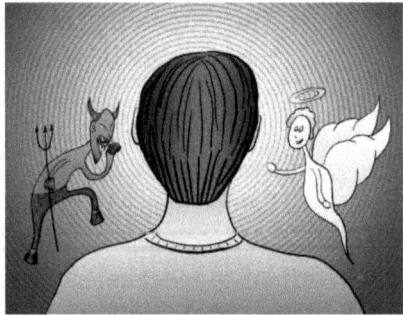

And also:

"Who shall separate us from the love of Christ? shall tribulation, or distress, or persecution, or famine, or nakedness, or peril, or sword?

Nay, in all these things we are more than conquerors through him that loved us.

For I am persuaded, that neither death, nor life, nor angels, nor principalities, nor powers, nor things present, nor things to come,

Nor height, nor depth, nor any other creature, shall
be able to separate us from the love of God,
which is in Christ Jesus our Lord."
(Romans 8: 35, 37-39)

If, after being purified from past sins, someone is in sin **just before** the return of the Lord, or if they die before repenting of that sin or while in the act of sin, the consequence when he/she appear before the Lord **will depend** on the type of "Christian" life he/she lived.

If for example, the person has lived their life in the fear of God, kept their testimony and obeyed the instructions of the Holy Spirit, this person has the assurance of knowing that the weight of the works of obedience in their life is greater than the fall into their last sin, for which reason the Lord shall say:

"Well done, thou good and faithful servant. Enter into the joy of the Lord" (Matt. 25:21)

Because our perfection **is not measured by how few times we have fallen into sin**, as we have seen the Bible declare: " if we say we have no sin, we deceive our own selves" (1 John 1:8); **but how we walk in obedience** to God and His Word, permitting the Holy Spirit to conclude His work of perfecting us.

We see this graphically:

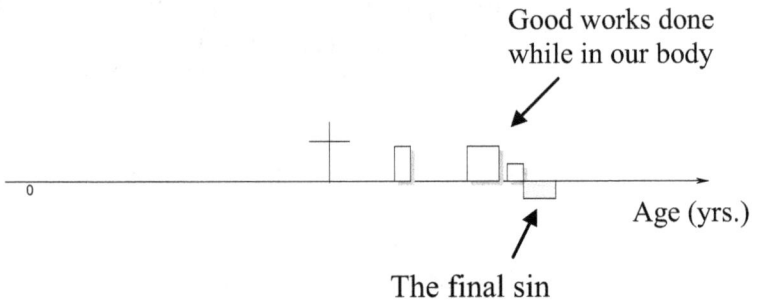

Nevertheless, this gives us no cause to abuse the grace of God, as the Bible strongly emphasizes:

"For **if we sin willfully after that we have received the knowledge of the truth**, there remaineth no more sacrifice for sins,

But a **certain fearful looking for of judgment** and fiery indignation, which shall devour the adversaries.

He that despised Moses' law died without mercy under two or three witnesses:

Of how much sorer punishment, suppose ye, shall he be thought worthy, who hath trodden under foot the Son of God, and hath counted the blood of the covenant, wherewith he was sanctified, an unholy thing, and hath done despite unto the Spirit of grace?" (Hebrews 10:26-29)

To "sin willingly" is the same as "rebellion".

That being so, if a person continually sins, after being purified of past sins, the weight of those sins is once again borne by their soul;

And if he/she dies in that condition and comes before the tribunal of Christ to be judged, if the weight of his/her sins is greater than the good works done, he/she **can be rejected**.

It can be illustrated like this:

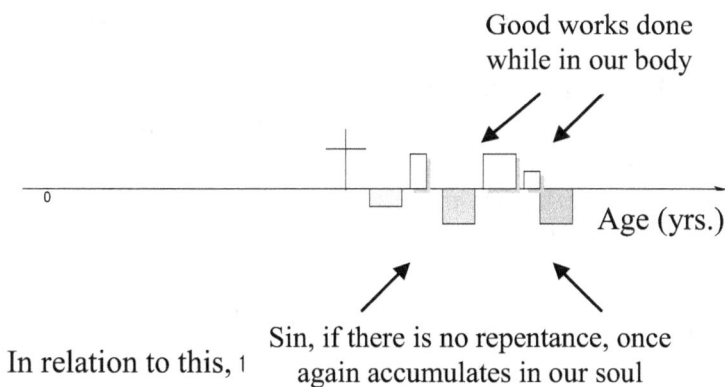

Good works done while in our body

Age (yrs.)

In relation to this, ₁

Sin, if there is no repentance, once again accumulates in our soul

"**Be not deceived; God is not mocked**: for whatsoever a man soweth, that shall he also reap.
     For he that soweth to his flesh shall of the flesh reap corruption; but he that soweth to the Spirit shall of the Spirit reap life everlasting"
(Gal 6:7-8)

"For we must **all** appear before the **judgment seat of Christ**; that every one may receive the things done in his body, according to that he hath done, **whether it be good or bad.**" (2Co. 5:10)

"And now, little children, abide in him; that, when he shall appear, we may have confidence, and **not be ashamed before him at his coming.**" (1John 2:28)

""Blessed are those who **wash their robes, that they may have the right to the tree of life** and may go through the gates into the city. (Revelation 22:14) *(NIV- New International Version of the Holy Bible)*

"**He that overcometh,** the same shall be clothed in white raiment; **and 1 will not blot out his name** out of the book of life, but I will confess his name before my Father, and before his angels." (Revelation 3:5)

The Bible also says:

"**Not every one that saith unto me, Lord, Lord**, shall enter into the kingdom of heaven; but **he that doeth the will of my Father** which is in heaven.

Many will say to me in that day, Lord, Lord, have we not prophesied in thy name and in thy name have cast out devils? and in thy name done many wonderful works?

And then will I profess unto them, I never knew you: **depart from me, ye that work iniquity."**

(Mathew 7:21-23)

"The LORD is slow to anger, and great in power, and **will not at all acquit the wicked:** the LORD hath his way in the whirlwind and in the storm, and the clouds are the dust of his feet" (Nahum 1:3)

"But why dost thou judge thy brother? or why dost thou set at naught thy brother? for **we shall all stand before the judgment seat of Christ.**
For it is written, As I live, saith the Lord, every knee shall bow to me, and every tongue shall confess to God. So then **every one of us shall give account of himself to God."**

(Romans 14:10-12}

This is **more serious** than we may realize at first glance.

Moreover: Concerning those that are believers for a season, and then abandon the way of the Lord, the Bible tells us that their situation is worst than before they became believers:

"For if after they have escaped the pollutions of the world through the knowledge of the Lord and Savior Jesus Christ, **they are again**

entangled therein, and overcome, **the latter
end is worse with them than the beginning**.

For it had been better for them not to have
known the way of righteousness, than, after they
have known it, to turn from the holy
commandment delivered unto them"
(2 Peter 2: 20-21)

We now reiterate, God cannot be mocked.

We should live conforming to the Word that assures us **a
true Christian is not in a revolving door, entering and
leaving the grace of God**; but is sure in the hands of God.

Now that "neither death, nor life, nor angels, nor
principalities, nor powers, nor things present, nor things to
come, nor height, nor depth, nor any other creature, shall
be able to separate **us from the love of God**, which is in
Christ Jesus our Lord" (Romans 8:38-39)

A sinful life is unnatural for the true Christian.

We may even call it "anti- natural". We can no longer
commit the same old sins. Having been born of the
Spirit, a believer is a new creature for which "*old things
have passed and all things have become new*"
(2 Corin. 5:17).

Our old life is past; **and though its dormant force may remain**, it is dominated and declared dead **by the new Presence** that abides in us (Romans 6:11).

That which before was a practice and habit, has now changed and becomes unnatural, and contrary to the new desires of our heart.

"He who is born of God," said John, "cannot sin (or continue in the practice of sin)." That is to say, sin is foreign to our new nature.

That which before was a practice and habit, has now changed and becomes unnatural, and contrary to the new desires of our heart

The nature that is ours by faith does not sin.

Who is in Control now?

Now, when the old nature regains control, temporarily and unexpectedly, our new man opposes this unnatural intrusion. We immediately turn to Christ.

The Bible tells us that though we be unfaithful to the Lord, He remains always faithful. He cannot deny himself. (2 Timothy 2:13)

The Lord is always there to intercede on our behalf before the Father (Hebrews 7:25), demonstrating his love for us will never fail.

When the believer who has sinned returns to Christ, he does not come with the desperation of a lost soul, but in full understanding that **as he is a child of God**, he has an Advocate with the Father, who is Faithful and Just, and will forgive our sin and cleanse us of all shame.

This is how the believer exercises his prerogative as a child of God, **without doubting his position** based on the knowledge of the infallible righteousness of Christ by faith.

Nevertheless, it is necessary to show the correlation between free will and our responsibility as believers, as God <u>never removes the ability to choose freely</u> when He receives us as his son/ daughter.

By the exercise of free will, the believer accepts salvation, and becomes a child of God; but should also be cautious and **not have a careless attitude toward sin**.

He cannot apply the grace of God as a license to sin. The Word teaches that our God, as He is **love** (1 John 4:16), is also a **consuming fire** (Deut. 4:24)

This is how the believer exercises his prerogative as a child of God

What shall we say then? Shall we continue in sin so that grace may abound? Paul asked (Romans 6:1)

"God forbid", was the answer (Rom. 6:2).

The answer is an **emphatic no**. Paul knew and taught that to practice sin adversely affects the faith of a believer; and faith is what makes our fellowship with God possible.

It is presumptuous, arbitrary, and an evidence of rebellion to continue in sin. To rebel is contrary to obedience demonstrated through faith.

Believers should be constantly vigilant

> "**Looking diligently** lest any man fail of the grace of God; lest any root of bitterness springing up trouble you, and thereby many be defiled"
>
> (Hebrews 12:15)

The exhortation of the Bible is:

> "**Examine** yourselves, whether ye be in the faith; **prove** your own selves" (2 Corin. 13:5)

BECAUSE:
> "Blessed is the man that endureth temptation: for when he is tried, he **shall receive the crown of life**, which the Lord hath promised to them that love him." (James 1:120)

Jesus tells us:

> "And, behold, I come quickly; and my reward is with me, to give every man according as his work shall be." (Revelation 22:12)

A final word of caution:

Let us live our life in a manner that enables us to appropriate the words of the Apostle Paul:

> "I have fought a good fight, I have finished my course, I have kept the faith:
> Henceforth there **is laid up for me a crown of righteousness**, which the Lord, the righteous judge, shall give me at that day: and not to me only, but unto **all** them also that love his appearing." (2 TIMOTHY 4:7-8)

We should live in the Truth and teach others only the Truth. We trust in God always, as He will never fail us.

Blessings and Peace.

From atheist to Pastor. A personal anecdote

As of the moment I am writing these lines I've passed the important age of fifty years old. After being taught the traditional Christian religion, I became an atheist in 1974, while in my sophomore year at the university.

After studies in philosophy; and being exposed to the depth of thought of the great philosophers; I accepted their teachings. I also perceived how there were very many contradictions even amongst them.

My mother, father, and a brother were Christians. I would mock them, argue vehemently with them, and spoke disparagingly of the pastor that would visit them, as I thought he was a deceiver. I hated to even hear the word "God."

Anger would flow through me when I heard that word. As I read and studied, if the author mentioned the word "God", I would immediately discard and even toss the book, considering it to be "junk."

I now remember as a child that whenever I would sneeze, my mother would say "God Bless You." Well, in those days I would ask my mother to stop saying those words to me as I had disdain for the word "God." I told my mother that since sneezing was the sign that my body was receptive to germs, she should say "Health" instead.

She departed to be with the Lord in 1978, three weeks after attending my graduation; with the pain of knowing her son was rebellious and she could not utter a blessing

For him. (But I could never stop her from praying for me when she had devotions; and I am sure God heard her prayers and in His time answered them)

I graduated as a Chemical Engineer in June 1978 and worked in my profession. I was able to develop and expanded the acquired knowledge in my specialty as an employee of all the companies that hired me.

Since I didn't believe in God, I had evolutionary beliefs, and sought in all science the answers to the questions my heart demanded. **I had disdain for the word "God."**

I had a particular definition of what God was. I believed:

> "God was a myth created by feeble and ignorant minds that had as a purpose, other than motivating people to become good citizens; comforting poor souls for their lack of competence or intellect. This vain illusion would compensate them for the failure in their lives, as after death they would live well."

For a long time, I sought to discover why things exist or occur as they do; for example, how is it the light and brightness of the sun continues for so many years without diminishing? Why does the force of gravity exist, is the universe without limits, or what causes the perfection of the atom, etc?

Who was the designer of that computer?

I would imagine the possibility of the existence of an advanced **computer** somewhere in the universe that controlled everything and designed gravity to stop the stars from colliding. Then the question would arise:

> Who designed and programmed that computer? Where was the mind behind such perfection in the universe?

I had so many questions and science was not satisfying my troubled mind (although I was then a technical consultant with my field of expertise being scientific and technical information; responsible for answering all the inquiries from professionals in all fields.)

In 1988, my older brother asked me if I had anyone I could consider as a best friend. I told him I had friends, but in the final analysis, I trusted no one. I considered myself alone. He invited me to a meeting where he would introduce me to someone that could be my best friend, and I would truly be able to trust.

I went to the meeting and saw it was held in a Catholic church where the catechism group and charismatic believers among them were presenting Jesus Christ.

I became somewhat frustrated with my brother, but remained there with him. The following Saturday the presentation would continue.

Many things occurred in my life during the next week and I was in anguish. When I opened the Bible I saw passages that spoke of judgment and destruction, but also other verses that spoke of God's desire to forgive me, that He loved me, etc.

I returned to the next meeting and felt more tranquil, although awaiting something. I continued attending the Catholic Church though I was ashamed to tell my neighbors and friends I now believed in God and Jesus Christ truly existed.

I immigrated to the United States in April 1990 intent on starting a consulting and importing business, which would make me a millionaire; but God had a different plan for my life.

Although I wanted nothing to do with other Christian sects (I called them Protestants in a demeaning manner or more cordially, our "separated brethren") in August of that year the Lord brought me to "New Life Fellowship" church and in December of that year I participated in water baptism.

I started serving Him, willing to allow His purpose to be fulfilled in me. The Lord has showed much to me and I am sure more will follow. I know I am in his hands, and I ask His perfect will be done in my life.

Know the love

As a person

The Manifestation of Love.

There is a force that moves all humanity. It is more powerful than electricity, conquers more than does money, and has a stronger pull than gravity.

This is the force of Love

It emanates from the source of all things created: GOD

His Word tells us that GOD wants to demonstrate HIS love to every person. This includes YOU. He tells you:

> "I drew you with cords of a man, with bands of love"   Hosea 11:4

These cords speak of a sacrifice, thru love, that made it possible to save YOU.

Maybe your ways are far from God, nevertheless, He seeks you to save you, bless you, prosper you, and above all have fellowship with you.

> "For God so loved the world that he gave his only begotten Son, that whosoever believeth in him should not perish, but have everlasting life"
> John 3:16

> "But God commendeth his love toward us, in that, while we were yet sinners, Christ died for us"
> Romans 5:8

Draw near to God. He is your Creator. Allow Him to save you. Do not resist the call of His love. It is very easy to receive the forgiveness of God, as Christ paid the price that was demanded.

Do your part now:

a) Recognize you are a sinner. You have not been perfect before God.

b) Repent for being away from God.

c) Ask for forgiveness with all your heart for all your transgressions.

d) Receive the grace of God in your life, salvation of your soul, confessing Jesus Christ as lord and Saviour.

e) Learn to live in God's will. To accomplish this, it is necessary to speak with Him (pray); Learn what God desires for you (read the Bible, attend a local church Where the Word of God is preached and taught.)

f) Share the love you have received from God with others.

The Lord says:

"Come now, and let us reason together, saith the LORD: though your sins be as scarlet, they shall be as white as snow; though they be red like crimson, they shall be as wool" (Isaiah 1:18)

"That if thou shalt confess with thy mouth the Lord Jesus, and shalt believe in thine heart that God hath raised him from the dead, thou shalt be saved" (Romans 10:9)

"If we confess our sins, he is faithful and just to forgive us our sins, and to cleanse us from all unrighteousness" (1 John 1:9)

"And the blood of Jesus Christ his Son cleanseth us from all sin" (1 John 1:7b)

Pray to God, ask His forgiveness for all of your sins and receive His grace and love.   **Blessings.**

If what you have read has been helpful to you, please thank and give ALL the glory to the Lord Jesus, for is He the only one who is worthy to receive it; and ask God for the next step you should do; **and Obey Him!**

A testimony

The testimony of Frank Mercado after finishing the translation of the book into the English language.

"I write these lines to inform you I was blessed as I read the concluding pages as the explanation of how we are called to live a holy life before God was inspiring". My goal now is to also inspire others, as I strive to inform and persuade them; and I believe you have achieved this all in your final chapter."

"He is the Comforter, who is God and lives in us (John 14:15-17), that leads us to all truth. I pray we do not repeat the mistakes of past movements that have been content with seeking the loaves of bread and the abundance of fish, as did the multitude. His mission is to bring all humanity to the knowledge of salvation through Jesus, our Messiah."

"I am convinced the book brings us to a more complete understanding of the grace and mercy of God, as well as being an interesting introduction to basic theology. Those of us who desire to become serious students of the Word of God will also be motivated."

"I finish by letting you know that the testimony concerning your mother has moved me, and I believe will bring a blessing to many souls."

"The peace of our God be to you and your family always."
****

What about YOUR testimony?

Other books Author has published:

The Missing Link – in Theology

In the book "The Missing Link - in Theology", the author examines the causes for so many divisions within the Christianity; and presents in a simple and enjoyable way, a deep analysis of some very conflicting topics that allows us to have a better understanding on the subject of salvation.

He also led us to discern a new "Tradition" that has corrupted the Christian message.

Among the questions analyzed, are:

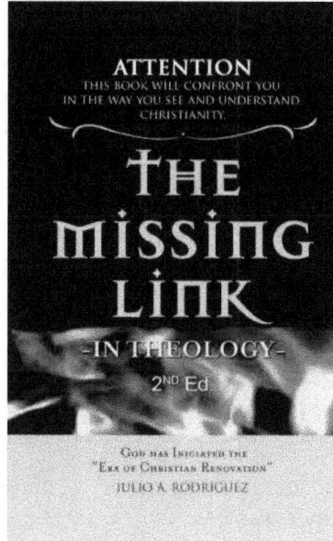

- What has happened with the Christianity?
- Why it seems that the lessons of the Bible had lost its force in this generation?
- What happens to a person that dies without receiving the Lord Jesus Christ as his personal Savior, if he has not heard the message of salvation? Will there be a remote possibility that God allows him to enter heaven?

"The Paradigm, or Tale? of Evolution"

In this book the author, a Chemical Engineer, ex-atheist and now Christian Pastor, demonstrates that "Evolution" is a **Dogma of Faith;** and the "Millions of Years" and the complexity of the subject of evolution, is only a subtle and dangerous maneuver to divert human attention from the true crucial point over the existence of the universe.

The Paradigm, or Tale?

of Evolution

A Christian-Scientific Research

2nd Edition

Julio A. Rodríguez

He also reveals that in school, our children receive an INDOCTRINATION that makes them become atheists. We are convinced that everyone should read that book and Act accordingly!

ATHEISM HAS NO FOUNDATION

Without mattering what a person believes or understands about his/her own existence, logic and reason within them disturbs and compels them to look for answers for the purpose of life; because it is obvious that their life is slowing passing by.

In this book, **wise expressions of God-believing great scientists** are presented; in contrast to the improbable myths that Atheistic Scientists declare.

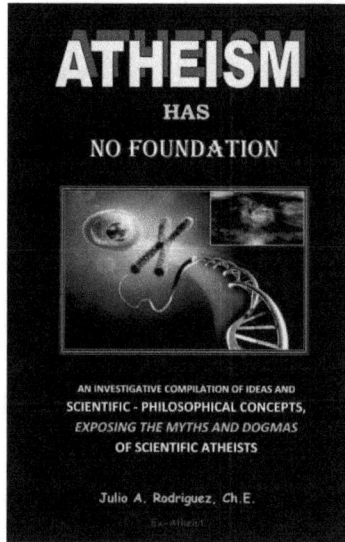

ATHEISM
HAS
NO FOUNDATION

AN INVESTIGATIVE COMPILATION OF IDEAS AND
SCIENTIFIC - PHILOSOPHICAL CONCEPTS,
EXPOSING THE MYTHS AND DOGMAS
OF SCIENTIFIC ATHEISTS

Julio A. Rodriguez, Ch.E.
Ex-Atheist

Due to the fact that the basic questions of life do not have satisfactory answers in Atheism, those that call themselves "Atheists" have resorted to the absurd rejection of verified facts, promoting fables disguised as scientific truths; and making pretentious unfounded declarations, attempting to calm and silence the conscience of everyone who asks a reason why they believe what they believe.

www.ingramcontent.com/pod-product-compliance
Lightning Source LLC
Chambersburg PA
CBHW060521030426
42337CB00015B/1965